MODERN DICTIONARY

FOR THE LEGAL PROFESSION

THIRD EDITION
2004 CUMULATIVE SUPPLEMENT

Gerry W. Beyer
Professor of Law
School of Law, St. Mary's University

William S. Hein & Co., Inc.
Buffalo, New York
2004

ISBN 0-8377-3036-8

Printed in the United States of America.

This volume is printed on acid-free paper by
William S. Hein & Co., Inc.

Contributors

Jeffrey Blackwell
Nanna Frye
Erik C. Greiner
Bertha Gutierrez
Janet Jackson
Renee R. Jaime
Nathan Ketterling
Jennifer A. Owens
Katharine L. Smith

PREFACE

The 2004 supplement to the third edition of *Modern Dictionary for the Legal Profession* contains more than five hundred new, updated, and revised terms which have been carefully selected to help the reader achieve the superior communication skills that are essential for success in the always challenging legal arena.

I hope my goal to provide you with modern and slang terms, as well as various legal terms, has been satisfactorily met in this supplement. If you decide to use one of the terms in your legal work, you should, as with any other authority, verify that the definition remains accurate and current.

If you have suggestions for additional terms or detect any errors, please let me hear from you. Your comments will be of great assistance in preparing supplements and future editions. Please direct your correspondence to:

Professor Gerry W. Beyer
School of Law
St. Mary's University
One Camino Santa Maria
San Antonio, Texas 78228-8603

GWB@ProfessorBeyer.com

Gerry W. Beyer
July 2004

A

Accredited Investor [update].
For a person and the person's spouse to be considered an accredited investor, they need joint income exceeding $300,000 per year for the prior two years along with a reasonable expectation that they will reach the $300,000 threshold in the current year.

Acknowledgment (definition 2) [update].
The notary must personally know the person giving the acknowledgment or must have sufficient evidence to ascertain the person's identity such as a driver's license or passport.

Acquired Immunodeficiency Syndrome [update].
As of 2002, approximately 886,575 Americans and 42 million people worldwide are afflicted with HIV. It is estimated that 3.1 million people died from AIDS in the year 2002.

Activa System [update].
The success rate of the Activa system is now approximately 90%.

Acute Care [update].
See Chronic Care.

Ad Hoc Arbitration.
Arbitration conducted on a case-by-case basis rather than by following established procedures and rules.
See Administered Arbitration; Arbitration [main volume].

Administered Arbitration.
Arbitration in which the arbitrator follows established procedures and rules.
See Ad Hoc Arbitration; Arbitration [main volume].

Advance Fee Fraud.
See 419 Fraud.

Adware.
Computer program which, often without the user's knowing consent, collects information about computer use which is sent to advertisers so they may direct targeted advertisements to the user via the Internet. Adware is a type of spyware.
See Keylogger; Spyware.

Aerostat [update].
In 2002, the United States was using both the Aerostat and ROTHR System.

African Franc [update].
The African Franc was linked to the Euro with a fixed exchange rate in 1999.
See Euro [main volume].

Ageline [update].
In 2002, Ageline contained more than 60,000 abstracts and content summaries of current literature on aging.

Agent Scrub [update].
The CIA has cut back the number of paid informants by at least 60%.

Agoraphobia [update].
Approximately 3.2 million Americans between the ages of 18 and 54 suffer from agoraphobia and 19 million suffer from anxiety disorders in general which include agoraphobia, panic disorder, obsessive-compulsive disorder, post traumatic stress disorder, generalized anxiety disorder, and phobias (social phobia, agoraphobia, and specific phobia).

Air Bag [update].
The phase-in of special air bags to protect SUV occupants in rollovers, called "smart" air bags, began in 2001. The National Highway Traffic Safety Administration proposed that 35% of all new passenger cars and light trucks should have smart air bags by 2003, 65% by September 2004, and standard in all new cars by 2005.

Airborne Laser [update].
The Airborne Laser aircraft has been developed and is undergoing flight-worthiness testing as of 2002. The laser system will be installed once testing is complete. The director of the airborne laser program, Col. Ellen Pawlikowski, hopes to conclude final airborne testing in which the laser fires upon a ballistic missile early in its flight, in 2004.

Airline Private Club [update].
Airline club fees now range from $225 to $500 per year. The clubs are becoming more crowded with average business travelers rather than upper class corporate travelers.

Air Rage [update].
The number of air rage incidents has decreased since 9-11.

See 9-11.

All-Terrain Vehicle [update].
Approximately 50,000 ATV riders are injured per year with 40% of them being children. Between 1982 and 2001, 1,714 children under 16 years of age were killed on ATVs. Of those, 799 were children under the age of 12.

All Writs Act [update].
The United States Supreme Court held in *Sygenta Crop Protection, Inc. v. Henson*, 123 S. Ct. 366 (2002), that the All Writs Act does not give federal courts the authority to remove state court cases even if the court's motive is to prevent the frustration of orders previously issued by the court.

Alternative Dispute Resolution [update].

See Collaborative Law.

Alternative Medicine [update].
In 2001, approximately 69% of Americans used some form of alternative health care.

Alternative Newspaper [update].
Between 1990 and 2002, the number of alternative weeklies increased from 68 to more than

100 and circulation soared from approximately 3 to 5 million.

Alzheimer's Disease [update].
Over 4.5 million individuals had Alzheimer's disease in 2003. The time of symptom onset to death averages around 8 years but can range from 3 to 20 years. Most individuals with Alzheimer's are diagnosed after reaching age 65 but symptoms may occur while the person is only in the 40s.

Amanuensis Rule.
Validation of the signature of a grantor's name on a deed when the signature is made by another person with the grantor's express authority but without having formal authority to sign on the grantor's behalf. The person signing the grantor's name is not considered an agent but rather is treated as a mere instrument or amanuensis of the grantor.

Amber Alert.
Rapid response system to locate a child who has been kidnapped. The alert is quickly broadcast over radio and television and posted on the Internet and electronic highway signs. The name derives from a kidnapping victim, Amber Hagerman, who was murdered by her kidnapper in 1996.

American Academy of Religion [update].
The American Academy of Religion had 9,000 members as of April 2003.

American Association of Retired Persons [update].
The AARP had a membership in excess of 33 million individuals as of 2002.

American Civil Liberties Union [update].
As of 2003, the ACLU had approximately 400,000 members and supporters with offices in almost every state.

American Foundation for Suicide Prevention [update].
More than 30,000 people in the United States die by suicide every year. It is this country's 11th leading cause of death.

American Municipal Bond Assurance Corporation [update].
Ambac received a AAA rating from Standard & Poor's Corporation in 1979.

American Society of Heating, Refrigeration and Air Conditioning Engineers [update].
ASHRAE had 55,000 members as of 2002.

Americans With Disabilities Act [update].
Approximately 52.6 million Americans had some type of disability as of 1997.

American Trucking Association [update].
ATA had 35,000 motor-carrier members as of 2002.

AmeriCorps [update].
Approximately 250,000 volunteers have served in AmeriCorps since its establishment.

Amnesty International [update].
As of 2003, there were more than 1.5 million members, supporters, and subscribers in more than 150 countries and territories in every region of the world.

Anaphylactic Shock [update].
Anaphylactic shock may be treated by an injection with a premeasured, prescription dose of epinephrine. Known as EpiPen or Ana-Kit (epinephrine), these self-administered medications are easily and rapidly injected into the thigh muscle. This is extremely effective and fast acting. Anyone who has experienced a prior anaphylactic reaction should carry these kits.

Anchoring [update].
See Neurolinguistic Programming.

Anencephaly; *Spina Bifida* [update].
The United States Public Health Service recommends that all women who could possibly become pregnant get 400 micrograms of folic acid every day. This could prevent up to 70% of some types of serious birth defects, including anencephaly and other neural tube defects.

Angioplasty [update].
Approximately 1,025,000 angioplasties were performed in the United States in 2000.

Animousity.
Repeated clicking of a mouse button on an Internet hyperlink with the usually false belief that doing so will increase the download speed of the next screen of material.
See Hyperlink [main volume]; Internet [main volume].

Anthelminic [update].
The correct spelling of this term is "anthelmintic."

Anthrax [update].
Use of the anthrax vaccine has increased. In 2002, medical experts from the Institute of Medicine concluded that the anthrax vaccine was sufficiently safe for use by United States military personnel. However, the experts do not believe that evidence of the vaccine's safety is sufficient to justify widespread inoculation of the public.

Antiarrhythmic [revised].
Drug which prevents or corrects an irregular heart beat.

Antibiotic [update].
Some studies have shown that up to 50% of the antibiotic prescriptions written by physicians are unnecessary.

Antioxidant.
See Flavonoid.

Antipersonnel Mine [update].
There are an estimated 200 million antipersonnel mines worldwide of which half are in place and half are in stocks. They are located primarily in the developing world. Plastics have largely displaced metal in antipersonnel mine manufacture. In some instances, almost no metals are used, so that many mines are virtually undetectable. In size, they can be as small as a human hand. They are cheap to produce; market rates for some mines are now as low as $3.00 per mine.

Apology Law.
Law restricting the use of a person's statements of sympathy or regret after an accident as evidence that the person was at fault for causing the accident. Approximately five states have apology laws.

Apostille.
Form used to authenticate documents, such as marriage and birth certificates, among nations that have joined the 1961 Hague Convention. The United States joined this Convention on October 15, 1981.

Application Service Provider; ASP.
Business which provides computer software, such as word processors and accounting programs, on the company's website. Individuals wanting to use these programs pay a fee and then access the programs via the Internet.

Arbitration [update].
See Administered Arbitration; Ad Hoc Arbitration.

Assisted Suicide [update].

Physician-assisted suicide bills were introduced in four states in 2003. Three of the bills, in Arizona, Hawaii and Vermont, called for legalizing the practice; while a North Carolina bill introduced by two physician legislators called for banning it.

ASP.
See Application Service Provider.

Asthma [update].
As of 2003, 20.3 million American report having asthma.

Atmosphere [update].
The stratosphere contains the ozone layer, the protective layer that filters out ultraviolet rays entering the lower atmospheres.

Automated Teller Machine [update].
Approximately 85% of banks collect fees from non-customers who use their ATMs.

Automatic Dialer.
Telephone device which automatically places calls so the caller does not have to dial individual numbers.
See Lead Generator; Predictive Dialer.

Axis of Evil.

Reference to the countries of Iran, Iraq, and North Korea coined by President George W. Bush in 2001 in response to their political policies which allegedly support terrorists and the acquisition of weapons of mass destruction. In 2002, the countries of Cuba, Libya, and Syria were added to the Axis of Evil.

B

B2B.
Acronym for *business-to-business* frequently referring to companies whose primary customers are other businesses.
See B2C.

B2C.
Acronym for *business-to-consumer* frequently referring to companies whose primary customers are consumers.
See B2B.

Baby Man [revised].
Person who illegally purchases a baby or child from a parent. The parent often uses the money received from the sale of the baby to purchase drugs.

Baby Moses Law.
Law permitting a parent of a young child to abandon the child at specified locations. These laws usually provide that if the parent delivers the child unharmed, the parent will not face prosecution for child abandonment. Texas enacted the first Baby Moses law in 1999 and at least thirty other states have done likewise. The name derives from the Biblical figure Moses who was abandoned as a child and watched over until he reached the hands of someone who was willing and able to provide appropriate care.
See Legalized Abandonment Law [main volume].

Band of Angels [update].
Band members have founded companies such as Cirrus Logic, Symantec, National Semi-Conductor, and Logitech, and have been executive officers at Sun Microsystems, Hewlett Packard, Intel, 3Com, and Intuit. Since 1994, Band members have placed more than $110 million into more than 140 startup companies.

Bar Code [update].
See Radio-Frequency Identification.

Bariatric Surgery [update].
Approximately 75,000 individuals underwent bariatric surgery in 2002, which is a 67% increase from 2001.

BASE Jumping [update].
There are approximately 10,000 BASE jumpers worldwide. BASE jumping usually is the cause of between 5 and 15 deaths each year.

Baskerville Effect.
Heart attack triggered by psychological stress. The term is derived from the book *The Hound of the Baskervilles* by Arthur Conan Doyle in which a character suffered a fatal heart attack after being exposed to a fear-inducing situation.

Bayesian Filter.
Computer program designed to eliminate spam. The program is based on a mathematical theorem named after Thomas Bayes, a

British mathematician and politician. By assigning a numerical value to key words in an e-mail message, the program determines the likelihood that the message is spam.

See Spam [main volume].

Bidi [update].

An increasing number of cities and states are banning or regulating the sale of bidis.

Biometrics.

Identification of a person which is based on a biological characteristic such as DNA, a fingerprint, or a retinal scan.

See Biometric Device [main volume].

Biopharm Crop.

Crop genetically engineered to contain particular chemicals which may then be used in vaccines or medicines. Advocates of this technique point to benefits such as cheaper and environmentally friendly production while opponents fear that dangerous substances could be inadvertently released into food products.

See Biotechnology [main volume].

Biotechnology; *Genetic Engineering* [cited].

The definition from the second edition was quoted in Andrew F. Nilles, *Plant Patent Law: The Federal Circuit Sows the Seed to Allow Agriculture to Grow*, 35 Land & Water L. Rev. 355, 355 (2000), and cited in Elisa Rives, *Mother Nature and the Courts: Are Sexually Reproducing Plants and Their Progeny Patentable Under the Utility Patent Act of 1952?*, 32 Cumb. L. Rev. 187, 188 (2001–2002).

See Biopharm Crop.

BIS Monitor.

See Bispectral Index [main volume].

Bisseur.

Person paid to attend a concert and call out for an encore at the end of the performance.

See Claque [main volume]; Rieur.

Bite and Hold.

Technique in which a police dog bites the suspect and holds him or her until a police officer subdues the suspect. Controversy exists whether this technique may be the unreasonable use of force, especially if the suspect was not given a prior warning or chance to surrender.

See Circle and Bark.

Black Friday.

Friday after Thanksgiving which, because of large sales occurring that day, is often the first day of the year when a retailer shows a profit for the year, that is, goes "into the black."

Black Tuesday.

The American stock market crash of October 29, 1929, which began the Great Depression.

Blawg.
Blog written by a lawyer.
See Blog.

Blind Plea.
Guilty plea of a defendant in a criminal case in which there is no previous sentencing recommendation arrangement with the prosecution.

Blocking.
Hunting practice in which one hunter stands at the end of a field or other area to prevent prey from escaping while other hunters shoot at the prey. This practice is extremely dangerous because the shooting hunters may inadvertently hit the blocking hunter.

Blog.
Personal diary posted on the Internet by the person who wrote it. The term is a shortened form the phrase "web log."
See Blawg; Internet [main volume].

Blood Alcohol Content [update].
As of 2002, fifteen states still used the .10 blood alcohol content threshold. Largely due to the efforts of Mothers Against Drunk Driving (MADD), the .08 threshold will become federal law on October 1, 2003. All states not in compliance will have 2% of their federal highway construction funding withheld. The withholding of funds will increase by 2% each year until 2006. All withheld funds will be returned to those states that pass the .08 threshold law by October 1, 2007.

Blood Bank [revised].
Organization which stores donated blood to be used by individuals requiring blood transfusions during surgical procedures. As a result of modern medical procedures, such as organ transplants, blood demand has increased significantly in the last decade at a rate of 4% per year. In 2002, the American Association of Blood Banks, along with the American Red Cross and other related organizations, joined together in a nationwide plea for blood donors as several regions faced critical blood shortages. Each day, an estimated 34,000 pints of blood are needed. Although 60% of the United States population is eligible to donate, only about 5% of Americans actually donate blood. The average blood donor is white, male, and over 35 years of age.

Bovine Spongiform Encephalopathy [update].
Bovine spongiform encephalopathy or "mad cow" disease is also known as "variant Creutzfeldt-Jacob disease."

Brady Bill [update].
Since the inception of the National Instant Criminal Background Check System mandated by the Brady Bill, approximately 976,000 of the 45.7 million background checks resulted in rejections.

Broadband.
Internet access which is significantly faster than dial-up service using telephone lines. Broadband technologies include DSL, cable, and T-1 lines.

Browse-Wrap Agreement.
Agreement found on a web-site or CD/DVD-ROM which the user is considered to have accepted even though the user has not expressly demonstrated consent by clicking on an "I agree" or "yes" icon. The enforceability of terms found in a browse-wrap agreement is uncertain.

See Click-Through Agreement.

Bumfights.
Fights between homeless individuals which are videotaped, copied, and then sold. Allegations exist claiming that these homeless individuals are offered food, alcohol, money, and lodging to participate in the fights. The sellers of these recordings, however, claim that most, if not all, of the fights are staged in a manner similar to professional wrestling.

Business Network International [update].
As of November 2002, BNI had more than 52,000 members in more than 2,600 chapters worldwide.

Bycatch [update].
Internationally, approximately 44 billion pounds of fish constitute bycatch every year.

Bypass Trust [update].
The amount which can pass without incurring federal estate tax for a death occurring in 2003 was $1,000,000. This amount increased to $1,500,000 in 2004.

C

CAFE.

See Corporate Average Fuel Economy Standards.

CAPTCHA.

Acronym for "Completely Automated Public Turing test to tell Computers and Humans Apart."

See Reverse Turing Test; Turing Test.

Carbon 14 Test [update].

This method is based on the assumption that once an organism dies it ceases to absorb carbon 14, which is found in the earth's atmosphere and the assumption that the amount of carbon in the atmosphere now is the same as it always has been.

Because carbon 14 decays at a constant rate, an estimate of the date the organism died can be made by measuring the amount of carbon 14 remaining in the sample. It is impossible to date rocks and minerals with carbon 14 methods. Only organic material, that is, plants and animals, may be subject to the carbon 14 tests, because they take in carbon 14 during their lifetimes.

Carbon Monoxide [update].

Legislation aimed at reducing carbon monoxide emissions has resulted in a fall in poisoning deaths. In 1970, the Clean Air Act was passed in the United States to reduce carbon monoxide. The use of catalytic converters in cars helps bring down the carbon monoxide content of exhaust fumes.

Researchers at the Centers for Disease Control and Prevention have been assessing the impact the Act has had on carbon monoxide mortality. They find a decrease of 21.3% in accidental deaths and 5.9% in suicides linked with carbon monoxide between 1975 and 1996. Nearly 12,000 deaths have been avoided since the introduction of the Act.

Carnivore; *DCS1000*.

Computer software used by the federal government to collect data contained in e-mail messages sent over the Internet. The government must first obtain a warrant before installing a device using the Carnivore software to monitor the targeted person's messages as they pass through an Internet service provider. Controversy exists over this software because of fears that the government could easily monitor e-mail messages of non-targeted individuals.

See E-mail [main volume]; Internet [main volume]; Internet Service Provider [main volume].

Cartagena Protocol of Biosafety [update].

As of September 2003, 46 countries have ratified the treaty, 21 countries have entered an accession to the treaty, and The

Netherlands has accepted the treaty.

Case of the Golden Buddha [update].

The Golden Buddha case has lost its status as the largest jury award in history. In 2002, a jury awarded $28 billion in punitive damages against Philip Morris, Inc. in favor of a former smoker with lung cancer. Albeit in a class action rather than in a suit by an individual, an even larger award in the amount of $145 billion was granted in 2001 in Florida against a group of cigarette makers. Both of these verdicts have been appealed and in December 2002, the judge reduced the award against Philip Morris to $28 million. In May 2003, an appellate court overturned the verdict in the class-action case holding that the case was improperly tried as a class-action lawsuit.

Catalyst Theory.

Theory which contends that a plaintiff is a prevailing party if the plaintiff's lawsuit is responsible for a voluntary change in the defendant's behavior even though the court does not award the plaintiff any specific relief. A plaintiff will attempt to use the catalyst theory to obtain an award of attorney fees as the victorious party. The United States Supreme Court in *Buckhannon Board & Care Home v. West Virginia*, 121 S. Ct. 1835 (2001), rejected the theory and held that under federal civil rights law, a prevailing party is entitled to attorney fees only if the court actually awards relief.

CCA.

See Chromated Copper Arsenate.

Celsius [update].

To convert a Fahrenheit temperature into Celsius: Tc = (5/9) * (Tf-32).

To convert a Celsius temperature into degrees Fahrenheit: Tf = ((9/5)*Tc) + 32.

Central and East European Law Initiative [update].

In 2000, CEELI received a grant from the Trust for Mutual Understanding to support its fellowship program for environmental lawyers from Central and Eastern Europe to study in the United States.

Certified Financial Planner [update].

As of 2003, there were approximately 65,000 Certified Financial Planners in the United States.

Certified General Appraiser [update].

A certified general appraiser must complete 180 hours of classroom training, pass a state test, and have two years' training experience.

Certified Residential Specialist [update].
More than 34,000 real estate agents held the CRS designation as of 2002.

Chain Consumer Price Index.
See Superlative Consumer Price Index.

Chalking.
Information and advertisement delivery method whereby a person uses chalk, often in a variety of bright colors, to write messages and draw pictures on sidewalks.

Charitable Lead Trust [update].
See Vulture Trust.

Charter School [update].
As of 2003, there were approximately 3,000 charter schools in thirty-six states and the District of Columbia. More than 700,000 students were attending these charter schools.

Checkbook Journalism [update].
In a 1995, California's checkbook journalism law was struck down as unconstitutional. The law, enacted in the wake of the O.J. Simpson trial, prohibited crime witnesses from selling their stories for a designated period of time.

Check Digit [cited].
The definition from the first edition was quoted in Eric Wymore, *It's 1998, Do You Know Where Your Medical Records Are? Medical Record Privacy After the Implementation of the Health Insurance Portability and Accountability Act of 1996*, 19 Hamline J. Pub. L. & Pol'y 553, 583 (1998).

China White [update].
"3-methylfentdnyl" should be "3-methylfentanyl."

C.H.I.P.S. [update].
This acronym also stands for Medicaid's low cost "Children's Health Insurance Program."

Choice of Evils Defense.
Defense to a criminal charge in which the defendant justifies the criminal act because the consequence of not committing the crime would be worse than the crime itself. For example, a car driver whose brakes fail may deliberately crash into a parked car rather than hit pedestrians. Controversy exists over whether this defense is effective with regard to the medical use of marijuana, that is, the person uses marijuana rather than suffer from severe pain.

Chromated Copper Arsenate; CCA.
Preservative used to pressure-treat lumber which protects it from rotting and insects. Because CCA contains arsenic, controversy exists over its safety and whether wood treated with CCA may cause arsenic poisoning or cancer.

Chronic Care.
Medical care for an ongoing condition over an extended period of time.
See Acute Care [main volume].

Circle and Bark.
Technique in which a police dog runs around the suspect while barking aggressively, but without actually biting the suspect, until a police officer subdues the suspect.
See Bite and Hold.

Civil False Claims Act; *Informer's Act; Lincoln Law* [update].
Congress passed the original Civil False Claims Act during the Civil War and it was signed into law by President Lincoln on March 2, 1863.

Click-Through Agreement.
Agreement found on a web-site or CD/DVD-ROM which the user accepts by clicking on an "I agree" or "yes" icon.
See Browse-Wrap Agreement.

Clitoridectomy [update].
It is estimated that approximately 135 million women have endured this procedure.

Closed Practice.
Service provider, such as a physician or attorney, who is not accepting new patients, clients, etc.

CNN Effect.
Live media coverage of events which makes it difficult for covert action to take place. The term is derived from the on-the-scene television coverage by the Cable News Network of important events such as the Gulf War in 1991.
See Gulf War [main volume].

Coach Class Thrombosis.
See Deep Vein Thrombosis.

Codeine Syrup; *Down; Drank; Lean; Nod.*
Prescription-strength cough syrup which is sometimes illegally used as a recreational drug. The drug acts as a sedative with drowsiness and confusion being common side effects.

Cognitor.
Proposed name for a prestigious global business credential to be awarded by the American Institute of Certified Public Accountants which would recognize the holder's skills in a variety of fields such as business law and accounting.
See American Institute of Certified Public Accountants [main volume].

COLI.
See Corporate-Owned Life Insurance.

Collaborative Law.
Alternative dispute resolution mechanism used to negotiate a settlement before litigation begins and without judicial supervision. The potential litigants and their

attorneys are encouraged to participate fully in this process. Collaborative law is especially popular in divorce cases.

See Alternative Dispute Resolution [main volume].

College Trust [update].
The Economic Growth and Tax Relief Reconciliation Act of 2001 provides that distributions from Section 529 plans are tax-free provided the distributions are used for certain educational expenses including tuition and fees, room and board, and books. Distributions for other purposes are taxed and the earnings portion of the distributions are subject to a 10% penalty.

Common Cause [update].
As of 2003, Common Cause had approximately 200,000 members.

Community Rating.
Health care insurance industry practice of determining rates based on the average cost of providing health care to individuals in a defined geographic area rather than by examining the individual characteristics of each insured such as age, medical condition, use of tobacco products, etc.

Comparative Advertising [update].
In *Pizza Hut, Inc. v. Papa John's Intern., Inc.*, 227 F.3d 489 (5th Cir. 2000), *cert. denied*, 532 U.S. 920 (2001), the court held that although Papa John's advertising campaign may have been deceptive, Pizza Hut did not have "sufficient evidence establishing that the misleading facts conveyed by the slogan were material to the consumers to which it was directed."

Compulsive Gambling Disorder; *Pathological Gambling* [update].
As of 2002, approximately 4.4 million Americans suffered from compulsive gambling disorder.

Concussion [update].
Approximately 82,000 brain injuries occur each year during recreational sports activities.

Confidential Marriage.
Marriage which is not generally discoverable from a search of the public records. Only the married individuals and individuals who obtain a court order with good cause may obtain a copy of the marriage certificate. This procedure is available in a few states and originated in the 1800s as a method of permitting couples who lived together without the benefit of marriage to get married without publicly revealing that they had not previously been married.

Congestive Heart Failure [update].
Nearly 5 million Americans are living with heart failure, and 550,000 new cases are diagnosed each year.

Consumer Price Index [update].
The CPI has been criticized as overstating inflation by at least

one percentage point annually. Suggestions have been made to make major revisions to the CPI or replace it with a more accurate cost of living index.

See Superlative Consumer Price Index.

Contingent Employee.

Employee, such as a temp, on-call worker, leased employee, or independent contractor, who works only when the employer has an immediate need for his or her services. Controversy may arise regarding the entitlement of a contingent employee to fringe benefits. Audrey Freedman, a labor economist, is often credited with coining this term.

Corporate Average Fuel Economy Standards; CAFE.

Government program established by the Energy Policy and Conservation Act in 1975 which mandates the average miles per gallon which passenger cars and light-duty trucks must attain.

Corporate-Owned Life Insurance; COLI; *Dead-Peasant Life Insurance.*

Life insurance policy purchased by an employer on a non-essential employee's life. A court may prohibit an employer from collecting on this type of policy because the death of the employee would not cause a financial hardship on the corporation and thus the corporation lacks an insurable interest in the employee's life. Instead, the corporation is "wagering" on the life of the employee with the expectation of obtaining a windfall upon the employee's death.

See Key Person Insurance (main volume).

Court Appointed Special Advocate [update].

As of 2003, there were more than 900 CASA programs in the United States with 70,000 persons serving as advocates.

Crack House [cited].

The definition from the first edition was quoted in Edward G. Renner, *Too Much (Legislation)Is Never Enough: Utilizing a Court's Equity Power to Enjoin Lawful Firearms Sales*, 32 J. Marshall L. Rev. 1225, 1227 (1999).

CTD.

See Cumulative Trauma Disorders.

Cumulative Trauma Disorders; CTD.

Generic reference to repetitive motion disorders such as carpal tunnel syndrome, trigger finger, tennis elbow, and golfer's elbow.

See Carpal Tunnel Syndrome [main volume].

Cyberchondria.

Imagined ailments triggered when a person susceptible to hypochondria researches medical symptoms and conditions using the Internet.

See Hypochondriasis [main volume].

Cybertrespass.

Unauthorized access or use of data stored on the Internet. Controversy exists regarding what types of data access and use will trigger tort liability for cybertrespass.

D

Danielle's Law.
Law providing that a person who murders a child in the child's home is eligible for the death penalty. The term is derived from a case involving the murder of a seven year old girl, Danielle van Dam, in 2002.

Data Mining [update].
New careers in data mining are emerging, as positions for data mining analysts and data mining engineers become available.

DCS1000.
See Carnivore.

Dead-Peasant Life Insurance.
See Corporate-Owned Life Insurance.

Deep Vein Thrombosis; DVT; *Coach Class Thrombosis; Economy Class Syndrome.*
Medical condition occurring when a blood clot forms in a person's lower leg and later breaks up which allows pieces to flow through the veins to the heart and lungs blocking blood flow and causing oxygen deprivation. In some cases, the pieces may reach the brain triggering a stroke. The condition may occur in airline passengers on long flights who have their legs in a downward position for an extended period of time. Controversy exists regarding whether airlines should warn passengers about DVT and recommend exercises to prevent the condition.

Defensive Attribution.
Coping mechanism in which a person blames the victim of a crime, disease, natural disaster, or some other event to create a psychological distance from the victim which then acts to minimize the person's fear of experiencing the same fate. For example, a person could blame the victim of a rape because the victim was provocatively dressed or was walking in a bad part of town late at night. Attorneys need to be aware of defensive attribution when presenting cases to juries.

Dengue Hemorrhagic Fever [update].
The World Health Organization estimates that approximately 50 million cases of dengue hemorrhagic fever occur each year, resulting in over 500,000 hospitalizations.

Depression [update].
As of 2003, approximately 18.8 million people in the United States suffer from depression.

Design Patent [update].
A design patent has a term of 14 years from the grant, and no fees are necessary to maintain a design patent in force.

Designated Settlement Fund; DSF.
Fund composed of structured settlement proceeds which obtains favorable federal income tax treatment by permitting the settling defendant to receive a tax deduction for the amount paid even if the fund does not distribute the money to the plaintiff in the same year. A DSF is similar to a qualified settlement fund but does not require continuing supervision of the court or government entity that created the fund. However, a QSF may be used for a greater variety of claims.
See Qualified Settlement Fund.

Designer Estrogen.
Drug developed to provide the benefits of estrogen but without the harmful side effects such as an increase in the risk of heart attack.
See Estrogen [main volume].

Dextromethorphan; DXM.
Drug commonly used in nonprescription cold and cough medicines. Because dextromethorphan may cause mind-altering effects at high dosages, products containing the drug are subject to abuse. As of January 2004, there were no legal restrictions on the purchase or sale of medicines containing DXM.

Diabetes Mellitus [update].
As of 2003, an estimated 15.7 million Americans have diabetes.
See Metabolic Syndrome.

Diagnostic and Statistical Manual of Mental Disorders [update].
The fifth edition of the DSM is not scheduled for publication until 2010 or later.

DIG.
Case originally accepted for review by the United States Supreme Court but later rejected with the notation that the writ of certiorari is "dismissed as improvidently granted."

Digital Divide [update].
The digital divide is narrowing at a relatively swift rate over recent years.

Diphtheria [update].
Between 1980 and 1999, only 49 cases of diphtheria were reported in the United States.

Direct Broadcast Satellite [update].
The number of DBS subscribers has significantly increased over the past few years to over 18 million subscribers in 2001. Analysts predict that 25 million people will be DB subscribers by 2005.

Doctor Shopping.
Practice of a patient complaining about the same ailment to different doctors to obtain multiple drug prescriptions. Substance abusers sometimes use this technique to obtain drugs. In some states, a person who doctor shops may be subject to criminal penalties.

Down.
See Codeine Syrup.

Down Syndrome [update].

Down Syndrome occurs in approximately 1 out of every 800 to 1,000 births.

Drank.

See Codeine Syrup.

Dresser-Drawer Deed.

Deed to real property which the grantor places in a dresser drawer or other location rather than delivering it to the grantee. Problems arise when this type of deed is located after the grantor's death because it is difficult to determine whether the property passes according to the terms of the undelivered deed or through the now-deceased grantor's estate.

Drug Court [update].

Nationwide, there are more than 800 drug courts in operation. By reducing jail use, drug courts save approximately $10 for every $1 spent on the program.

DSF.

See Designated Settlement Fund.

DVD [update].

A double-sided DVD disk holds 9.4GB of data. Many companies are working on a new type of disk which would be recorded with a blue laser beam enabling the disk to hold upwards of 27GB of data.

DVT.

See Deep Vein Thrombosis.

DXM.

See Dextromethorphan.

Dynamic Pricing.

Retail merchandising practice of setting the price for an item based on a consumer's income or previous buying habits.

E

Early College High School.
High school designed to enhance the success of students (especially disadvantaged students) by providing college-level work during the student's junior and senior years.

Ebola Virus [update].
An experimental vaccine is being developed as of July 2003. A fast-acting version of the Ebola vaccine builds protection against the deadly virus in one month instead of the usual six and could make containment of the pathogen more realistic.

Economy Class Syndrome.
See Deep Vein Thrombosis.

Ecotourism [update].
The United Nations designated the year 2002 as the "International Year of Ecotourism." A study released in 2002 by the Travel Industry Association of America and National Geographic Traveler identified 55 million Americans as ***geotourists***, the researchers' term for ecotourists.

Ecstasy; MDMA [update].
An Ecstasy tablet in the United States costs from $40 to $70. Effects of Ecstasy may last up to six hours. In 2000, more than 6.4 million people age 12 and older reported that they have used ecstasy at least one time. Ecstasy use among teenagers has increased over the past few years and the perceived availability of the drug among teenagers has risen from 40% in 1999 to 50% in 2000.

e-Filing.
Filing of papers, such as tax returns and legal documents, over the Internet.
See Internet [main volume].

861 Position.
Claim that § 861 of the Internal Revenue Code relieves Americans from paying federal income tax on wages. Proponents of this position assert that only individuals employed by foreign-owned companies are required to pay federal income tax. Courts have consistently rejected the 861 Position.
See Pure Trust.

e-Lawyering.
Providing legal services to clients over the Internet or via e-mail.
See e-Mail [main volume]; Internet [main volume].

Electronic Signatures Act.
See Federal Electronic Signatures in Global and National Commerce Act.

e-Mail [update].
The number of e-mail messages sent each year is rising at a very rapid rate.

Employment Non-Discrimination Act [update].
The Employment Non-Discrimination Act (ENDA), H.R. 2692, was introduced July 31, 2001.

Enhanced Life Estate Deed; *Lady Bird Deed.*

Deed in which the holder of the life estate also retains the right to transfer the property, by sale or gift, without obtaining the consent of the owner of the remainder interest. If the life estate holder transfers the property, the remainder interest is destroyed unlike with a traditional life estate where the life estate owner cannot transfer more than his or her life interest without the consent of the holder of the remainder interest. Enhanced life estate deeds are sometimes called Lady Bird deeds because President Johnson allegedly used this type of deed to convey property to his wife.

Ensign Amendment.

Federal law passed in 1996 which effectively banned pornography in prisons. The law was upheld against claims that it was an unconstitutional violation of First Amendment free speech rights in *Amatel v. Reno*, 156 F.3d 192 (D.C. Cir. 1998), *cert. denied*, 527 U.S. 1035 (1999).

Ephedra [update].

In December 2003, HHS Secretary Tommy G. Thompson announced that the Food and Drug Administration (FDA) issued a consumer alert on the safety of dietary supplements containing ephedra and notified manufacturers of its intent to publish a final rule on dietary supplements containing ephedrine alkaloids. The rule will state that dietary supplements containing ephedrine alkaloids present an unreasonable risk of illness or injury. The rule would have the effect of banning the sale of dietary supplements containing ephedrine alkaloids when it becomes effective, 60 days following publication.

e-Philanthropy.

Donations made to charitable organizations via the Internet.

See Internet [main volume].

Epilepsy [update].

As of 2002, approximately 50 million people worldwide and 2.5 million Americans suffer from epilepsy.

E-Sign.

See Federal Electronic Signatures in Global and National Commerce Act.

Estonia [update].

As of July 2003, the population of Estonia was more than 1.4 million people.

Estrogen [update].

See Designer Estrogen.

ETF.

See Exchange-Traded Fund.

Ethical Will.

Statement of an individual's values, morals, ideas, advice, or recommendations designed to be read by family members and friends after the individual's death. The concept of the ethical will is based on the story of Jacob found in the Torah.

See Torah [main volume].

Ethics 2000 [update].

The Ethics 2000 committee submitted its first report to the ABA's House of Delegates at the ABA's August 2001 Annual Meeting. At subsequent meetings, the report has been debated and amendments have been made to the Model Rules of Professional Conduct.

Euro [update].

The following nations had adopted the Euro as of 2003: Austria, Belgium, Finland, France, Germany, Greece, Ireland, Italy, Luxembourg, The Netherlands, Portugal, and Spain.

European Patent Convention [update].

As of November 2003, EPC member nations included Austria, Belgium, Bulgaria, Cyprus, the Czech Republic, Denmark, Estonia, Finland, France, Germany, Greece, Hungry, Ireland, Italy, Liechtenstein, Luxembourg, Monaco, the Netherlands, Portugal, Romania, Slovakia, Slovenia, Spain, Sweden, Switzerland, Turkey, and the United Kingdom. There are also four EPC extension states, that is, Albania, Latvia, Lithuania, and Macedonia.

In the United States, for applications filed on or after June 8, 1995, utility and plant patents are granted for a term which begins with the date of the grant and usually ends 20 years from the date the person first applied for the patent subject to the payment of appropriate maintenance fees. Design patents last 14 years from the date the applicant is granted the patent. Patents in force on June 8 and patents issued thereafter on applications filed prior to June 8, 1995 automatically have a term that is the greater of the twenty year term discussed above or seventeen years from the patent grant.

European Union [update].

The 25 member states of the EU as of May 1, 2004, included Austria, Belgium, Cypress, Czech Republic, Denmark, Estonia, Finland, France, Germany, Greece, Hungary, Ireland, Italy, Latvia, Lithuania, Luxembourg, Malta, the Netherlands, Poland, Portugal, Slovakia, Slovenia, Spain, Sweden, and the United Kingdom.

Exchange-Traded Fund; ETF.

Index mutual fund which is traded on financial exchanges in a manner similar to traditional stocks and bonds. Investors often use ETFs to avoid paying the capital gains tax which is triggered when excessive redemptions occur on traditional mutual funds.

See Index Fund [main volume].

Exclusionary Rule [update].

The complete citation to the *Mapp* case is *Mapp v. Ohio*, 367 U.S. 643 (1961).

Exer-commuting.
Practice of engaging in a physical activity, such as walking or biking, as a means of getting to work rather than driving a car or taking public transportation.

Exon-Coats Communications Decency Act [update].
The complete citation to the *Reno* case is *Reno v. American Civil Liberties Union*, 521 U.S. 844 (1997).

Extreme Turbulence.
Violent air turbulence in which an aircraft is very difficult, if not impossible, to control.
See Light Turbulence; Moderate Turbulence; Severe Turbulence.

F

419 Fraud; *Advance Fee Fraud; Nigerian 419 Scam.*
Scam in which the con artist solicits financial assistance to get a large sum of money out of Nigeria. The fraud is usually perpetrated by e-mail, fax, or mail. In exchange for supplying funds allegedly needed for legal fees, taxes, and bribes, the scam artist promises the mark a significant share of the money. The scam is named after Section 419 of the Nigerian Criminal Code which prohibits the removal of funds from Nigeria.

420.
Slang reference, pronounced "four-twenty," for the smoking of marijuana.

Federal Electronic Signatures in Global and National Commerce Act; *Electronics Signature Act; E-Sign.*
Federal statute enacted in 2000 providing that electronic records and electronic signatures will satisfy the requirements for many writings and signatures under federal law.

Fibrin Sealant [update].
In 1998, the FDA approved fibrin sealant, and in 2000, the FDA approved an application device for fibrin sealant use.

Final Contact.
Touching the body of a deceased individual to confirm the reality of his or her death and to begin the process of accepting the person's death. This physical contact is an important step in the grieving process. If final contact is inappropriately denied to a family member, some courts may be willing to award the survivor emotional distress damages.

Financial Industries Modernization Act of 1999.
See Gramm-Leach-Bliley Act.

Flash Mob.
Gathering of individuals for no particular purpose coordinated by the mass distribution of messages containing the meeting date, time, and location via cellular telephones, e-mail, or Internet sites.

Flavonoid.
Chemical found in plants which may have a variety of health benefits including the reduction of heart attacks and the prevention of cancer. Flavonoids are a type of antioxidant.
See Antioxidant [main volume].

Flexible Spending Account; FSA.
Tax savings strategy by which an employer deducts a predetermined amount from an employee's pre-tax pay and places it in a special account which the employee may then draw upon to reimburse health care and dependent care expenses. Contributions to a FSA are exempt from federal income tax and social security tax. The employee may not recoup any excess contributions and thus the employee must be certain to

expend the amount in the account before the end of the plan year.

Flipping.
Unscrupulous practice of purchasing a house at a low price and then selling it at a price in excess of its actual value by misrepresenting the condition of the house to the purchaser.

Floppy-Infant Syndrome.
Medical condition in which a newborn child is extremely tired and has difficulty sucking. The condition may be caused by the mother's overuse of anti-anxiety drugs.

Food Wreck.
Slang term for a motor vehicle accident caused by the driver being distracted by eating or drinking while actually driving.

Freshman 15 or 25.
Slang reference to the syndrome of college students gaining 15 or 25 pounds during their first year in college due to poor eating habits and overindulgence in fast food and alcohol.

Freudian Slip; *Slip of the Pen; Slip of the Tongue* [cited].
The definition from the second edition was quoted in *Commonwealth v. Johnson*, 700 N.E.2d 270, 272 (Mass. App. Ct. 1998).

Friendly Parent.
Parent in a child custody dispute who asserts that he or she will support the child's relationship with the other parent. A judge may be more likely to award custody to a parent who appears willing to permit the child to have a relationship with the non-custodial parent. Controversy exists regarding the wisdom of this approach because a judge may overlook other equally or more important factors such as child abuse.

Frisk [update].
The complete citations to the *Terry* and *Wardlow* cases are as follows: *Terry v. Ohio*, 392 U.S. 1 (1968) and *Illinois v. Wardlow*, 528 U.S. 119 (2000).

Front Pay [revised].
Damages recovered in an employment discrimination lawsuit for lost future earnings either (1) between the date of the judgment and when the employee is reinstated or (2) in lieu of reinstatement. In 2001, the United States Supreme Court held in *Pollard v. E.I. DuPont de Nemours & Co.*, 121 S. Ct. 1946 (2001), that front pay is not subject to the compensatory damages cap provided under the Civil Rights Act of 1991.

Fry.
See Wet.

FSA.
See Flexible Spending Account.

Functional Food.
Food containing added ingredients known to prevent disease or pro-

Functional Food.

Food containing added ingredients known to prevent disease or promote health such as orange juice fortified with calcium. Controversy exists when a manufacturer adds herbs or other ingredients with unsubstantiated health benefits to a product and then advertises the product as if the health claims are accurate.

G

Gastric Band.

Band surgically placed around the upper part of a patient's stomach to enhance the ability of the patient to lose weight by causing smaller portions of food to create a long-lasting full feeling.

Generation D(igital).

Individuals belonging to Generation X or Generation Y who have expertise in technology matters. This generation is based more on an attitude embracing technology rather than chronological age.

See Baby Boomer [main volume]; Generation X [main volume]; Generation Y [main volume]; GI Generation [main volume]; Greatest Generation; I Generation [main volume]; Sandwich Generation [main volume].

Generation X [revised].

Individuals born between approximately 1965 and 1978. Characteristics often attributed to these individuals include a short attention span, desire for immediate gratification, insecurity, bitterness, and a greater emphasis on home and family life than professional accomplishments.

See Baby Boomer [main volume]; Generation D(igital); Generation Y [main volume]; GI Generation [main volume]; Greatest Generation; I Generation [main volume]; Sandwich Generation [main volume].

Generation Y; *Echo Boomer; Millennial* [revised].

Individuals born since approximately 1979. Characteristics often attributed to these individuals include computer literacy, familiarity with the Internet, significant spending on consumer goods, and the ability to influence family purchase decisions on items such as cars and computers.

See Baby Boomer [main volume]; Generation D(igital); Generation X [main volume]; GI Generation [main volume]; Greatest Generation; I Generation [main volume]; Sandwich Generation [main volume].

Geographic Profiling.

Method of determining the perpetrator of a series of crimes based on the assumption that serial criminals tend to commit their crimes close to where they live.

See Gang Profile [main volume].

Geotourist.

See Ecotourism.

Ghoul Trust.

See Vulture Trust.

Ginseng [update].

Harvested ginseng root had a selling price of between $250 and $500 per pound, and sometimes up to $700 per pound, as of 2002.

Global Gag Rule.

See Mexico City Policy.

God Squad (definition 2).

Endangered Species Committee, a cabinet-level committee that determines when economic concerns outweigh the protection mandated by the Endangered Species Act, and has the power to exempt specific sites from the act.

Gramm-Leach-Bliley Act; *Financial Industries Modernization Act of 1999.*

Act repealing statutes which had prevented banking, securities, and insurance industries from providing each other's services. The act also requires financial institutions to inform their customers of the institutions' policies regarding protecting customer privacy. Because of the broad definition the Federal Trade Commission has ascribed to the term "financial institution," attorneys who engage in a variety of activities such as tax and financial planning may need to provide clients with the required disclosures.

Greatest Generation.

Individuals who reached adulthood between the start of the Great Depression (1929) through the end of World War II (1945).

See Baby Boomer [main volume]; Generation D(igital); Generation X [main volume]; Generation Y; GI Generation [main volume]; I Generation [main volume]; Sandwich Generation [main volume].

Greenpeace [update].

As of 2002, Greenpeace had 250,000 United States members and 2.8 million members worldwide.

Groundhog Day Opera.

Reference to the Telecommunications Act of 1996 and the annual reports thereunder which was coined by Prof. Thomas W. Hazlett.

See Regional Bell Operating Company [main volume].

Ground Zero.

Former location of the World Trade Center buildings in New York City which were destroyed when two passenger jets commandeered by terrorists crashed into them on September 11, 2001.

See 9-11.

Gulf War [update].

See CNN Effect.

H

Habitat for Humanity [update].
As of 2003, Habitat has built more than 150,000 houses around the world, providing more than 750,000 people in more than 3,000 communities with safe, decent, affordable shelter.

Hacker [update].
See Script Kiddie.

Harlem Shake.
Dance involving precision shaking of the dancer's shoulders, hips, and legs often attributed to having originated with the dancing of Al Boyce.
See Hip-Hop Generation [main volume].

Hart-Scott-Rodino Antitrust Improvements Act; *HSR Act.*
Federal law, 15 U.S.C. § 18a, which authorizes agencies that enforce antitrust laws to investigate and review potentially anticompetitive merger and acquisition transactions.

Hasty Pudding Theatricals.
Oldest undergraduate dramatic organization in the United States which is located at Harvard University.

Health Maintenance Organization [update].
See Indemnity Insurance Plan.

H5N1 Virus [update].
In 2001, poultry stalls in three Hong Kong markets were closed due to the H5 virus, which resulted in over 750 chicken deaths. The Secretary for the Environment and Food for Hong Kong assured the public that the samples collected from the infected stalls did not contain the same strain of H5N1 chicken virus that affected Hong Kong in the late 1990s causing human casualties.

Hilton Humanitarian Prize [update].
In 2003, the Hilton Humanitarian Prize was awarded to the International Rehabilitation Council for Torture Victims.

Hip-Hop Generation [update].
See Harlem Shake.

Hobson's Choice.
Choice between two alternatives in which there is only one realistic or viable choice because the alternative is nothing. The term is based on the alleged practice of livery keeper Thomas Hobson (England, 1544–1630) of requiring customers to choose between taking the horse closest to the door or no horse at all.

Honey Pot.
E-mail account created merely for the purpose of attracting junk e-mail to assist computer programmers to write programs to filter out spam.
See Spam [main volume].

Hospitalist.
Doctor who specializes in treating patients who are in the hospital. Hospitalists work along with the patient's primary care doctor and specialist to assist hospitalized

patients. The number of hospitalists is growing rapidly in the United States. This increase in use has lead to significant shortening of hospital stays as well as the lowering of hospital costs.

Hot Spot.

Location, such as a store, restaurant, or school classroom, where the Internet may be accessed using Wi-Fi.

See Wireless Fidelity.

HSR Act.

See Hart-Scott-Rodino Antitrust Improvements Act.

Huntington's Disease [update].

Recent research shows that production of certain mutant proteins in the brain by the renegade gene may have a part in the brain cell death experienced by these individuals.

I

ICANN.

See Internet Corporation for Assigned Names and Numbers.

IIS.

See Inflation-Indexed Security.

Illy.

See Wet.

Inattention Blindness.

Reduced ability to recognize and react to situations because an individual is distracted. The term is often used to describe a vehicle driver's lessened attention to driving while using a cellular telephone.

Indemnity Insurance Plan.

Health insurance plan which permits the insured to see any physician the insured desires but which requires the insured to pay for the services and then submit a claim for reimbursement to the insurance company. The amount of the reimbursement will depend on the terms of the insurance policy.

See Health Maintenance Organization [main volume].

Independent Practice Association; IPA.

Group of physicians who, although not practicing together, form a legal entity which enables them to contract with managed health care organizations.

Inflation-Indexed Security; IIS.

New name for a treasury inflation-protection security which better reflects how the security operates because the owner of the security is still responsible for income tax on the inflation adjustment.

See Treasury Inflation-Protection Security [main volume].

Informer's Act.

See Civil False Claims Act [main volume].

Instant Runoff Election.

Voting method in which voters rank candidates for each office in order of preference to eliminate the need for a separate runoff election. If no candidate gets a majority of the votes using each voter's first-place vote, the candidate who received the fewest number of votes is eliminated and the second-place votes of those voters are used. This process continues until a candidate receives a majority. Although used in only a few jurisdictions in the United States, such as San Francisco, the technique is popular in other countries including Ireland and Australia. A voter initiative to provide for instant runoff elections in statewide elections was defeated in Alaska in 2002.

Intangible Tax.

Tax imposed by some states on the ownership of intangible property such as stocks, bonds, and mortgages.

Intensive Care Unit; ICU [cited].
The definition in the first edition was cited in the case of *In re Commitment of N.N.*, 679 A.2d 1174, 1182 (N.J. 1996), and Lisa M. Yennella, *Liberty and Due Process Rights—Standard Governing the Involuntary Commitment of Minor Children Dictates that the Minor Must Suffer from Childhood Mental Illness, etc.*, 7 Seton Hall Const. L.J. 959, 975 (1997).

Inter-Governmental Panel on Climate Change [update].
One function of the IPCC is to provide periodic assessments of the state of knowledge on climate change. The Second Assessment Report in 1995 contained input, which led to the Kyoto Protocol 1997. The Third Assessment Report was completed in 2001, and the IPCC has agreed to complete the Fourth Report in 2007.

See Kyoto Protocol [main volume & supplement].

Inter-Governmental Philatelic Corporation [update].
The IGPC employs a full time staff, which includes researchers, graphic designers, and in-house artists, as well as more than 300 freelance artists to produce stamps for more than 60 countries.

International Campaign to Ban Land Mines [update].
In 1997, it was estimated that there were approximately 110 million buried land mines scattered throughout 68 countries. In 2003, it was reported that more than 52 million stockpiled antipersonnel mines have been destroyed, the number of countries producing them has decreased from more than 50 to 15, and there have been no significant exports of antipersonnel mines since the mid-1990s. 136 countries have ratified or acceded to the 1997 Mine Ban Treaty, and another 12 countries have signed but not yet ratified the treaty.

International Rescue Committee [update].
In May of 2003, the IRC entered Iraq to support internally displaced persons and rehabilitate school sanitation systems. The IRC also restores water treatment plants and village water networks, rehabilitates damaged or looted health clinics, trains primary health care staff, and performs child needs assessments.

International Skating Union; ISU.
Governing organization of speed skating, short track speed skating, figure skating, and synchronized skating. The ISU was founded in 1892.

Internet [update].
In August 2003, the national average of Internet usage by adults was 59%.

Internet Corporation for Assigned Names and Numbers; ICANN.
Non-profit corporation formed in 1988 by the Department of Com-

merce that administers the Internet's domain name system.

See Domain [main volume]; Internet [main volume].

Interpol [update].
As of January 2004, Interpol has 181 member countries.

In Vitro Fertilization [update].
The success rate of in vitro fertilization is approximately 29% per egg retrieval which is slightly greater than the 20% success rate a reproductively healthy couple has in achieving pregnancy.

IPA.

See Independent Practice Association.

ISU.

See International Skating Union.

J

Jefferson Muzzle [update].
Among the 2003 winners of the Jefferson Muzzle award were United States Attorney General John Ashcroft and the 107th United States Congress.

Joe Account.
Computer account in which the user name and password are the same. An unauthorized person may readily obtain access to this type of account.

Joe-Jobbing.
Spam e-mail technique in which the spammer uses another person's e-mail address or domain name to make the junk message look important or from a trustworthy source.

See Spam [main volume].

Jury Nullification [update].
In November 2002, the voters of South Dakota defeated an initiative which would have allowed a defendant to admit guilt and then argue to the jury that the law is unfair and that the defendant should consequently be acquitted.

K

Keyhole Surgery [update].
The world's first triple bypass surgery using keyhole surgery was performed in New York in 1997. Keyhole surgery is now FDA approved.

Keylogger; *Snoopware.*
Computer software which surreptitiously records every keystroke made by a computer user. This information may then be used to obtain confidential information about the user and the user's computer activities.
See Adware; Spyware.

Key Person Insurance [update].
See Corporate-Owned Life Insurance.

Kimmel's Index.
See K-Index.

K-Index; *Kimmel's Index.*
Mathematical formula developed by Joe Kimmel which is used to determine the likelihood that a vehicle will roll over during an accident.

Kye [cited].
The definition was cited and quoted, in part, in *Cho v. Chi*, 2002 WL 454302, *1 (Cal. Ct. App. 2002).

Kyoto Protocol [update].
As of the end of 2002, 101 countries (but not the United States) had ratified the Kyoto Protocol. The Protocol is expected to take effect in 2003 once the Russian Federation ratifies the Protocol.

L

Lady Bird Deed.

See Enhanced Life Estate Deed.

La Regla Lucumi.

See Santeria.

Laser Assisted Intrastromal Keratomileusis [update].

LASIK received FDA approval in 1995.

Latvia [update].

As of July 2003, the population of Latvia was approximately 2.4 million.

Law School Admission Test; LSAT.

Standardized examination which almost all law schools in the United States require as part of the application process. The half-day test consists of multiple-choice questions designed to evaluate the test taker's skills in analytical reasoning, logical reasoning, and reading comprehension. The exam also contains an ungraded essay question. Graded essay questions may be included in future versions of the LSAT.

Lead Generator.

Telephone device often used by telemarketers which automatically places calls and then plays a recorded message

See Automatic Dialer; Predictive Dialer.

Lead Poisoning [update].

Lead-based paints were banned for use in housing in 1978. However, the Center for Disease control reported in 2003 that approximately 24 million housing units in the United States have deteriorated leaded paint and elevated levels of lead-contaminated house dust. Over 4 million are homes to one or more young children.

Lean.

See Codeine Syrup.

Legalized Abandonment Law [update].

See Baby Moses Law.

Legal Realism [cited].

The definition in the first edition was quoted in Michael Rustad & Thomas Koenig, *The Supreme Court and Junk Social Science: Selective Distortion in Amicus Briefs*, 72 N.C. L. Rev. 91, 101 (1993).

Legal Services Corporation [update].

Congress provided $336 million in funding to the LSC for fiscal year 2003.

Life Settlement.

Third party purchase of a life insurance policy in exchange for the purchaser's right to be the irrevocable beneficiary of the policy as well as the policy owner. A life settlement is similar to a viatical settlement but does not require the insured to be in a terminal condition. Because the purchaser will probably need to wait a longer time to collect on the policy, the amount the insured receives is substantially less.

See Viatical Settlement.

Light Turbulence.

Mild air turbulence which causes an aircraft passenger to slightly strain against his or her seat belt. A passenger may walk with little or no difficulty during light turbulence.

See Extreme Turbulence; Moderate Turbulence; Severe Turbulence.

Lincoln Law.

See Civil False Claims Act [main volume].

Longer Combination Vehicle [update].

Heavy truck crashes are responsible for approximately 5,000 deaths and 130,000 injuries in America each year.

LSAT.

See Law School Admission Test.

Lyme Disease [update].

Approximately 23,000 people in the United States suffered from Lyme disease in 2002.

M

Maggie's Law.
Law which provides severe penalties for killing someone while driving a motor vehicle in a sleep-deprived condition. The law is named after Maggie McDonnell who was killed in 1997 by a driver who admitted not sleeping for 30 hours.

Magnetic Levitation [update].
The Federal Railroad Administration selected seven project corridors for studies of maglev technology in 1999. As of January 2001, the FRA selected the Baltimore-Washington corridor project as one of two project corridors to be considered for future maglev technology implementation. In 2003, the FRA will select the project corridor which will receive funds for the design and construction of maglev. Funding for the maglev project will come from federal, state, and local sources, both public and private.

Magnetic Resonance Imaging; MRI [cited].
The definition from the 1998 supplement was quoted in *Gamata v. Allstate Ins. Co*, 978 P.2d 179, 181 (Haw. 1999).

Mandated Benefits.
Health care benefits which state law requires all group insurance policies to contain.
See Mandated Offerings.

Mandated Offerings.
Health care benefits which state law requires all group insurance companies to offer to the business, company, or organization sponsoring the policy.
See Mandated Benefits.

Margin [cited].
The definition from the first edition was cited in *Han v. Commissioner*, T.C. Memo. 2002-148, n.4 (2002).

Markman Hearing.
Court procedure for the construction of the terms of a patent claim. The term is derived from the case of *Markman v. Westview Instruments, Inc.*, 517 U.S. 370 (1996), in which the Court determined that patent claims are to be interpreted by the court rather than by a jury.

Mary Carter Agreement [update].
The term derives from the case of *Booth v. Mary Carter Paint Co.*, 202 So. 2d 8 (Fla. App. 1967).

Massachusetts Trust.
Business technique in which investors grant management authority to a "trustee" and then receive certificates representing their investments. A Massachusetts trust is similar to a limited partnership and is not related to a traditional trust.

Matching.
See Mirroring.

MDMA.
Abbreviation for Methylene Dioxy MethAmphetamine, commonly known as Ecstasy.
See Ecstasy.

Medallion Signature.
See Securities Transfer Agents Medallion Program [main volume]; Securities Transfer Association [main volume]; STAMP [main volume]; STAMP Medallion [main volume]; Transfer Agent [main volume].

Medium Earth Orbit Satellite [update].
The first MEO satellite was successfully launched in 2001 from Cape Canaveral.

Megan's Law [update].
In *Smith v. Doe*, 538 U.S. 84 (2003), the United States Supreme Court held that a state may require a sex offender to register even if the crime was committed prior to the enactment of the state's Megan's law. The ex post facto prohibition of the United States Constitution was not violated because the law was nonpunitive and thus its retroactive application was permitted.

In *Connecticut Department of Public Safety v. Doe*, 538 U.S. 1 (2003), the United States Supreme Court determined that the due process clause of the United States Constitution does not require a hearing to determine whether an offender is currently dangerous before the individual's name may be included in a sex offender registry which is publicly disseminated.

Mercosur [update].
The European Union is committed to assisting Mercosur achieve its ambition of becoming a real common market.

Metabolic Syndrome.
Obesity-related medical disorder resulting which leads to an increased risk of heart attack, stroke, and diabetes. Typical symptoms of metabolic syndrome include high blood pressure, elevated blood sugar levels, and high cholesterol levels.
See Diabetes Mellitus [main volume]; Stroke [main volume].

Metadata.
Data contained in computer files, especially word processing documents, in addition to the information shown on the screen. Examples of metadata include previous versions of the file, information about the author, dates created and edited, hidden text, and internal comments. Persons are often unaware of the additional information revealed when they share computer files with others.

Metatag.
Key words describing the contents of a website inserted into the non-displayed portion of a website to increase the likelihood of the website being located by Internet

users who rely on search engines to locate desired sites. Controversy exists over the practice of a business inserting a metatag describing a competing business or product in an attempt to reach individuals who are not actually searching for the business's website.

Methamphetamine [update].

See Ya Ba.

Mexico City Policy.

Policy of the United States Agency for International Development which prohibits the funding of family planning services in other nations if they provide or advocate abortion. The term derives from the introduction of these restrictions at the 1984 International Conference on Population which was held in Mexico City.

Mice Print.

See Mice Type.

Mice Type; *Mice Print.*

Important terms in an advertisement, contract, or other document which are printed in a small hard-to-read font.

Microsite.

Internet site designed to be online for only a short period of time, usually as a method of promoting a particular event or product.

See Internet [main volume].

Mifepristone [update].

In 2001, more than 500,000 women opted to use the drug and approximately two-thirds of Planned Parenthood centers offered mifepristone as an abortion alternative.

Miller Trust.

Qualified income trust used in Medicaid planning which derives its name from the case of *Miller v. Ibarra*, 746 F. Supp. 19 (D. Colo. 1990). This technique was subsequently codified in 42 U.S.C. § 1396p(d)(4)(B).

See Qualified Income Trust.

Miranda Warning [update].

The citation to the *Miranda* case *is Miranda v. Arizona*, 384 U.S. 436 (1966).

Mirroring; *Matching.*

Neurolinguistic programming technique in which the user (attorney) attempts to put a person (juror or witness) at ease by mimicking that person's body language (e.g., hand gestures, posture, head position).

See Anchoring [main volume]; Neurolinguistic Programming.

Missing in Action [update].

As of September 2003, the Department of Defense reported the number of MIAs from recent wars is as follows: World War I = 3,350; World War II = 78,750; Korea War = 8,100; Cold War = 126; Vietnam War = 1,882.

MIST.

Acronym for Minor-Impact Soft-Tissue. MIST is used as a term of art in a lawsuit in which the victim of a relatively minor accident claims to have relatively severe injuries that are not objectively verifiable because only soft-tissue is involved.

MLP.

See Multijurisdictional Practice.

MMR Vaccine.

Single vaccine designed to protect against measles, mumps, and rubella.

Moderate Turbulence.

Air turbulence capable of causing an aircraft passenger to feel a definite strain against his or her seat belt. Walking during moderate turbulence is difficult.

See Extreme Turbulence; Light Turbulence; Severe Turbulence.

Modern Portfolio Theory.

Investment strategy used to obtain a specified rate of return while at the same time reducing the risk of the investment. The investor evaluates the success of the investment based on the return of the entire portfolio rather than on the performance of each individual asset.

Mother Hubbard Clause (definition 2).

Provision in a court decree stating that all relief not expressly granted in the order is denied.

Mothers Against Drunk Driving [update].

In 2002, 17,419 people were killed in crashes involving alcohol, representing 41% of the 42,815 people killed in all traffic crashes, according to National Highway Traffic Safety Administration (NHTSA) data.

Motor Voter [update].

In 2001, of the 8 million voters who registered using the motor voter law, only about 5% actually voted.

Mule (definition 2).

Coin which mistakenly has a different denomination imprinted on each side, e.g., the front of the coin looks like a penny while the reverse looks like a dime. A legitimate government-stamped mule is extremely valuable to coin collectors.

Multidisciplinary Practice [update].

In July 2000, the American Bar Association rejected the concept of multidisciplinary practice stating that attorneys should not share fees with non-attorneys and non-lawyers should not own or control businesses which engage in the practice of law

Multijurisdictional Practice; MJP.

Ability of an attorney or other professional to practice in a jurisdiction other than the jurisdiction in which the individual is licensed.

Multiple Sclerosis [update].

As of December 2003, more than 400,000 Americans and 2.5 million individuals worldwide have MS.

Must-Carry Law.

The citation to the *Turner* case is *Turner Broadcasting System, Inc. v. F.C.C.*, 520 U.S. 180 (1997).

N

Narcissistic Personality Disorder [update].
Approximately 1% of the general population suffers from this disorder.

National Association of Certified Valuation Analysts [update].
As of 2003, there are approximately 5,000 members.

National Association of Legal Assistants [update].
As of 2003, approximately 18,000 legal assistants have joined.

National Teaching Certificate [update].
As of 2002, there are approximately 24,000 teachers in the United States who have received national teaching certificates. The certification fee is now $2,300.

Nazi Speed.
See Ya Ba.

Neurolinguistic Programming; NLP.
Form of psychological therapy that instructs patients how to change their thoughts, feelings, and actions by mental exercises. Some attorneys use NLP techniques to influence or manipulate jurors and witnesses.
See Anchoring [main volume]; Mirroring.

News Robot.
Small motorized vehicle containing video and audio transmitting and receiving equipment which may be sent by remote control into dangerous areas permitting the news media to have access to locations which would be off-limits to human reporters such as war zones and areas affected by natural disasters.

New York Stock Exchange [update].
The NYSE now trades more than 2,800 listed companies.

Nigerian 419 Scam.
See 419 Fraud.

9-11.
Terrorist attacks on the United States which occurred on September 11, 2001 when (1) two passenger jets crashed into the World Trade Center in New York City leading to the collapse of the two towers shortly thereafter, (2) a passenger jet crashed into the Pentagon, and (3) a passenger jet crashed in rural Pennsylvania after the passengers apparently prevented the hijackers from steering the plane into their intended target.
See Air Rage [update]; Ground Zero.

NLP.
See Neurolinguistic Programming.

Nod.
Slang term for codeine syrup which comes from the street language term of art "to go on the nod"

which refers to the cycle of waking and sleeping caused by the drug.
See Codeine Syrup.

Noncommissioned Officer [update].
Enlisted person who holds the rank of Petty-Officer and above in the United States Navy and Coast Guard or Sergeant and above in the Marine Corps or United States Army. Non-Commissioned officers may earn commissions as officers if they complete the requirements for conferral of a bachelor's degree.

No Pay, No Play.
Law preventing uninsured vehicle owners from recovering non-economic damages. Approximately five states have no pay, no play statutes. Controversy exists over the wisdom of denying recovery to persons merely because they or the vehicle's owner was uninsured.

North Atlantic Treaty Organization [update].
In 2002, Russia became a limited partner as a member of the NATO-Russia Council.

O

Oath [update].
An oath is normally taken in front of an official, such as a judge or notary, and is accompanied by formalized gestures such as raising the right hand or placing the left hand on a book of religious significance such as the Bible.

Obsessive-Compulsive Personality Disorder [update].
It is now thought that more than 2% of the general population is afflicted with this disease.

Occam's Razor.
Theory that when litigants advance conflicting theories to explain an event, e.g., an accident or injury, the jurors are more likely to accept the simpler theory. This principle was part of the philosophy advanced by William of Occam in the early 14th century.

OGIT.
See Oil and Gas Investment Trust.

Oil and Gas Investment Trust; OGIT.
Trust which invests in and manages oil and gas property and in which investors may purchase interests. The development and recognition of these trusts, analogous to real estate investment trusts, is in the beginning stages.
See Real Estate Investment Trust [main volume].

1031 Exchange; *Starker Trust.*
Transaction in which the owner of investment property sells the property and then purchases within a short period of time other investment properties without incurring capital gains tax on the profit made upon the sale of the original property. These transactions are governed by Internal Revenue Code § 1031.

Operation Candyman.
Federal Bureau of Investigation operation conducted in 2002 to apprehend individuals involved in Internet-based child pornography. This FBI operation led to the arrests of 63 perpetrators.

Opiophobia.
Reluctance of physicians to prescribe opium-based drugs for pain management. A doctor's failure to treat a client for pain using opioids or other drugs may be malpractice.

Opus Dei [update].
More than 85,000 members and 1,800 priests are included in the membership rolls.

Oral Cancer [update].
Oral cancer affects more than 30,000 people and kills approximately 8,000 Americans per year.

Orphan Disease.
Disease which afflicts a small number of individuals and thus does not receive as much funding to discover a treatment or cure as more widespread ailments.

P

Panspermia.
Theory that life on earth began from microbes that originated off of the earth and which were brought here by, for example, comets and meteorites. The theory was originally propounded by Fred Hoyle, a British astronomer.

Papworth Cocktail.
Combination of three drugs which may be given to a brain-dead individual to help preserve the person's organs for transplant use. The drugs used in a Papworth Cocktail include hydrocortisone, vasopressin, and tri-iodothyronine.

Pareto Optimality [cited].
The definition from the first edition was cited in *R.S.M., Inc. v. Alliance Capital Management Holdings, L.P.*, 790 A.2d 478, 483 (Del. Ch. 2001).

Parkinson's Disease [update].
More than one million Americans now suffer from this disease.

Parthenogenesis.
Development of an egg into an embryo without the egg first being fertilized by sperm. Obtaining stem cells by using parthenogenetic eggs may avoid ethical problems with stem cell research because parthenogenetic eggs do not produce offspring.

See Cord Blood [main volume].

Partial Birth Abortion [update].
In the case of *Stenberg v. Carhart*, 120 S. Ct. 2597 (2000), the Supreme Court of the United States held that a Nebraska statute which criminalized the performance of partial birth abortions violated the United States Constitution. The Court left open the possibility that a more narrow statute might be constitutional if it contained an exception for the preservation of the health of the mother.

Pathological Gambling.

See Compulsive Gambling Disorder.

Pavlovean Reaction [update].
The correct spelling of this term is "Pavlovian Reaction."

Personal Financial Specialist [update].
As of 2003, there were approximately 2,500 certified specialists.

Person of Interest.
Individual whom a law enforcement agency believes has knowledge which would be helpful to solving a case. A person of interest is more vague than the term "suspect" which usually refers to someone whom law enforcement believes participated in a crime. Controversy exists whether the term is merely a euphemism for "suspect." Use of the term gained popularity after Attorney General John Ashcroft used it to refer to Steven Hatfill with regard to his

possible connection to unsolved incidents involving the mailing of anthrax to various individuals.

Petty Officer [update].
Non-commissioned officer in the United States Navy or Coast Guard.

Pharmaceutical and Personal Care Pollutants.
Contaminants which originate in food, household, and personal care products such as perfumes, over the counter and prescription drugs, personal hygiene and beauty products, insect repellants, coffee, and cigarettes. Studies reveal that rivers and lakes often have high levels of these pollutants.
See Over the Counter [main volume].

Phishing.
E-mail scam in which the culprit sends an e-mail message purporting to be from a company with which the victim does business. The e-mail requests the victim to update his or her account records by clicking on a link contained in the e-mail. The link leads to a web site which mimics the company's real site. The victim then provides credit card numbers, passwords, and other private information to the scammer.

Pink Ghetto.
Law school legal writing programs in which a majority of the instructors are female. Some individuals believe this fact is a result of gender discrimination.

PIPE Transaction.
See Private Investment in Public Equity Transaction.

Posse Comitatus Act.
Federal law originally enacted in 1878 which restricts the United States military from enforcing civilian laws unless expressly authorized by Congress or the Constitution. The Act is codified in 18 U.S.C. § 1385.

Potted Plant Rule.
Custom of the non-deposing attorney in a deposition to remain silent except to make objections.

PPLI.
See Private Placement Life Insurance.

Pragmatism [cited].
The definition from the first edition was cited in Ruthann Robson, *The Politics of the Possible: Personal Reflections on a Decade at the City University of New York School of Law*, 3 N.Y. City L. Rev. 245, 245 (2000).

Predictive Dialer.
Telephone device which automatically calls numbers and screens out numbers which are busy, answered by machine, disconnected, or are not answered. The device "predicts" when a dialed number is actually answered by a person and then transfers the call to a human caller. Predictive

dialers are in heavy use by the telemarketing industry and are often the focus of complaints because if a human caller is not available when the machine transfers the call, the call recipient is disturbed by a call without a person to whom to speak.

See Automatic Dialer; Lead Generator.

Pre-Impact Fear.

See Pre-Impact Fright [main volume].

Pre-Impact Fright [update].

Recovery for pre-impact fright is now allowed by most states if physical consequences or impact actually occurs.

Premenstrual Dysphoric Disorder [update].

Approximately 5% of menstruating women have this disorder.

Presbyopia [update].

An estimated 90 million Americans suffer from farsightedness as of 2002.

Presidential Library [update].

President Clinton's materials are collected in Little Rock, Arkansas at the William J. Clinton Presidential Materials Project.

Priftin.

See Tuberculosis.

Private Investment in Public Equity Transaction; *PIPE Transaction.*

Method of investment in which the investor guarantees his or her ability to resell the securities in the public market.

Private Placement Life Insurance; PPLI.

Life insurance policy in which the insured negotiates directly with the insurance company to enhance the terms of the policy.

Pump and Dump.

Scheme in which a person owning stock in a particular corporation makes false reports of inside information to encourage investors to buy stock in that corporation. These purchases artificially inflate the price of the stock after which the person sells the stock at a significant profit.

See Inside Information [main volume].

Pure Trust; *Sovereign Pure Trust.*

Trust which allegedly relieves individuals from their obligations to pay federal income tax based on the proposition that the 16th Amendment to the United States Constitution lacks an enabling clause and thus Congress does not have the authority to impose an income tax on individuals. The Internal Revenue Service views pure trusts as tax avoidance scams and federal authorities often prosecute promoters of these plans.

See 861 Position.

Pushing the Value.

Overstatement of the value of a house for sale which makes it easier for prospective purchasers to obtain financing. However, the practice results in higher monthly payments for the purchaser and hence a greater risk of default. If the property is sold at a foreclosure sale, there is an increased chance that the sale will be at a loss resulting in the purchaser being liable for the deficiency.

Q

Qualified Income Trust; QIT.
Method of shielding income from Medicaid qualification rules which is permitted under 42 U.S.C. § 1396p(d)(4)(B). A QITs is often used when an individual lacks sufficient income to pay for nursing home care but yet has income too great to qualify for Medicaid.
See Miller Trust.

Qualified Settlement Fund; QSF.
Fund composed of structured settlement proceeds which obtains favorable federal income tax treatment by permitting the settling defendant to receive a tax deduction for the amount paid even if the fund does not distribute the money to the plaintiff in the same year. A QSF is similar to a designated settlement fund but requires continuing supervision of the court or government entity that created the fund. However, a QSF may be used for a greater variety of claims.
See Designated Settlement Fund.

Queen for a Day Agreement.
Limited use immunity agreement under which a person agrees to provide information in exchange for the government's promise that any statements made will not be used against the person for any purpose.

QIT.
See Qualified Income Trust.

QSF.
See Qualified Settlement Fund.

R

Radio-Frequency Identification; RFID.

Process of using small transponders (tags) to transmit identifying information. A scanner or other type of device acts as an antenna which triggers the RF tag to transmit information. Common uses of this rapidly growing technology include monitoring merchandise in a store to reduce theft and charging the owners of vehicles as they pass through toll booths. RF tags often work better than bar codes because no close visual contact is needed between the scanner and the tag. Critics of RFID fear that tags could be surreptitiously inserted in products or clothing to track a person's movements.

See Bar Code [main volume].

Rave [update].

See Ya Ba.

Reduction-in-Force; RIF.

Business technique of reducing the number of employees usually to save money. A business may assert that employees are being fired because of reduction-in-force when in actuality the business's motive is to discriminate against employees based on age or some other impermissible ground.

Registered Nurse [update].

A registered nurse may hold either a Bachelor's or an Associate's degree.

Rent-to-Own [update].

Approximately three million people spend $6 billion annually in 8,300 rent-to-own stores in the United States.

Retrograde Extrapolation.

Method of determining a person's blood alcohol content at a particular time in the past (for example, when an automobile accident occurred) based on the amount of alcohol in the person's blood at a later time. Controversy exists regarding the accuracy of the technique.

Reverse Mortgage [update].

Reverse mortgages often provide for monthly payments which, along with interest, increases the balance of the loan. The amount of the payments depend on the life expectancy of the borrower; the older the borrower, the larger the payments. However, no repayments are needed provided the borrower is alive and remains in the home. When the borrower dies or moves out, then the balance is due.

Reverse Turing Test; *CAPTCHA*.

Computer technique which permits access to data only when the user completes a task which a human finds easy to complete but which is difficult for a computerized system to perform automatically. For example, the user may be asked to enter a password which is provided on the same screen but which is found within a picture rather than as computer-readable text. The computer may then ascertain that the user is indeed human and permit access to the information. The acronym CAPTCHA stands for "Completely Automated Public Turing test to tell Computers and Humans Apart."

See Turing Test.

RFID.

See Radio-Frequency Identification.

Rieur.

Person paid to attend a comical theatrical production and laugh.

See Bisseur; Claque [main volume].

RIF.

See Reduction-in-Force.

Rifapentine.

See Tuberculosis.

Right of Sepulture.

Right of a person to be buried or to have his or her cremated remains kept in a certain location such as a burial plot. In some states, a spouse has the right of sepulture in a plot owned by the other spouse. Also in some states, a spouse and children may have the right of sepulture in a deceased spouse's or parent's plot even if the plot is left by will to another person unless the will makes express reference to the plot.

Roach Bait.

See Undercover Marketing.

Robotard.

Person who abuses nonprescription drugs containing dextromethorphan.

See Dextromethorphan, Syrup Head.

Roth IRA [update].

United States Senator William Roth, for whom the Roth IRA was named, died in December 2003 at the age of 82.

Rule of Osha.

See Santeria.

S

Safe Return Program [update].
As of 2002, approximately 90,000 people were registered and there have been more than 7,000 safe returns since the program began in 1993.

Santeria; *La Regla Lucumi; Rule of Osha* [update].
Approximately 5 million people in the United States and more than 20 million people in Latin America practice Santeria.

Sarbanes-Oxley Act of 2002.
Extensive amendments to the federal law regulating corporate governance, disclosures, accounting practices, and penalties for violations which were enacted in response to corporate scandals.

Satellite Search and Rescue Network [update].
As of 2002, the Satellite Search and Rescue Network has saved more than 15,000 lives.

Schizophrenia [update].
More than 2 million Americans and over 60 million people worldwide suffer from schizophrenia.

School Voucher [update].
In 2002, the United States Supreme Court held in the case of *Zelman v. Simmons-Harris*, 122 S. Ct. 2460 (2002), that Ohio's Pilot Project Scholarship Program does not violate the Establishment Clause of the United States Constitution because the program is neutral in all respects toward religion and confers educational assistance directly to a broad class of individuals defined without reference to religion.

Script Kiddie.
Computer hacker lacking the sophistication to develop his or her own hacking programs. Instead, the script kiddie uses software developed by others to gain illegal access to computer systems.
See Hacker [main volume].

Second-Parent Adoption.
Adoption by one partner in a same-sex relationship of the child of the other partner. State laws vary regarding the recognition of second-parent adoption.

Separate But Equal Doctrine [update].
The citations to the *Plessy* and *Brown* cases are as follows: *Plessy v. Ferguson*, 163 U.S. 537 (1896) and *Brown v. Board of Education*, 347 U.S. 483 (1954).

Sepulture.
See Right of Sepulture.

Serbonian Bog.
Situation from which there appears to be no means of extrication. The term is derived from on a bog between Egypt and Palestine which appeared to be solid land because of blowing sand and in which armies were said to have been lost in ancient times.

Severe Turbulence.
Air turbulence which causes an aircraft to be temporarily out of control. Passengers are forced roughly against seat belts and walking is impossible.
See Extreme Turbulence; Light Turbulence; Moderate Turbulence.

Sickle Cell Anemia [update].
As of 2001, approximately 70,000 Americans have sickle cell anemia.

Slamming [update].
The Federal Communication Commission enacted strict anti-slamming rules applicable to slamming violations that occur on or after November 28, 2000.

Slot Walking.
Using coins, tokens, or credits abandoned by another person to gamble on slot machines. Casinos discourage this practice claiming that these items actually belong to the person who left them behind or the casino. Litigation may be necessary to determine whether the finder or casino has the superior claim to the property.

Sludge Syndrome.
Set of medical ailments allegedly caused by exposure to treated human waste used as fertilizer or land fill.

Smart Air Bag [update].
The NHTSA proposes that 25% of all new passenger cars have the smart air bag by 2003, with all new cars and trucks equipped by 2005.

Smoker's Lung.
Slang term for chronic obstructive pulmonary disease.
See Chronic Obstructive Pulmonary Disease [main volume].

Snoopware.
See Keylogger.

Snowflake Syndrome.
Proposition that no two particular items are the same, just like no two snowflakes are identical. The snowflake syndrome provides the basis for identification via fingerprints and DNA evidence. Controversy exists whether other things which could lead to the identification of individuals, such as ear or lip prints, are similarly reliable.

Sole Commissioner Government [update].
As of 2001, eleven of the 159 counties in Georgia have sole commissioners.

Sovereign Pure Trust.
See Pure Trust.

Spam [update].
See Bayesian Filter; Joe-Jobbing; Honey Pot.

Split Bond.
Procedure allowed in some states whereby an arrested person may

satisfy the dollar amount of the bond by combining a personal recognizance bond (no sureties or security) with a surety bond.

Split Dollar Life Insurance [update].
The validity of split dollar life insurance arrangements has been called into question by the passage of the Corporate Responsibility Act of 2002 which bans corporate loans to employees. The Treasury Department issued rules governing these policies in 2003.

Sport Utility Vehicle [update].
In 1999, 63% of deaths in SUV accidents were caused by rollovers. It is estimated that there were approximately 70,000 SUV rollovers resulting in 2,000 deaths in 2002. As a result, car manufacturers have begun to install specially designed air bags to protect the vehicle occupants in rollovers.

Spreading.
Allocation of the interest and other loan fees over the life of the loan. The determination of whether a loan is usurious is often computed by spreading. Interest and fees which may be permissible for the original term of a loan may become usurious if the term is shortened such as by an acceleration.
See Acceleration Clause [main volume].

Spyware.
Computer software which tracks how a computer is used and then surreptitiously transmits that information to others without the user's permission. A computer user may not be aware that spyware is running. Computer programs exist which can detect and remove spyware.
See Adware; Keylogger.

Stale Will.
Will which should be revised to reflect changes in the testator's circumstances such as births, adoptions, deaths, marriages, divorces, and the acquisition or loss of property, or applicable law such as construction rules and estate taxes.

Starker Trust.
See 1031 Exchange.

Starter Marriage.
First marriage of a person which typically lasts only a few years and which ends in divorce prior to the birth of children to the marriage.

Steganography.
Process of embedding a secret message in a digital video, audio, or picture file. A computer program subtlety alters the file which is then widely distributed such as by posting on the Internet. A person with the key may then extract the message.

Stella Award.
Lawsuit which is outrageous, ridiculous, or frivolous. The term was coined after a New Mexico jury awarded Stella Liebeck $2.9 million for injuries suffered after she spilled a hot cup of coffee on herself at a McDonald's restaurant. Many lawsuits reputably deserving

of the Stella Award are fabricated or are urban legends.

See Urban Legend.

Stem Cell.

See Parthenogenesis.

Stop Loss Insurance.

Insurance coverage which protects an uninsured or self-insured person or organization from paying claims in excess of an amount stated in the policy.

Strategic Petroleum Reserve [update].

The SPR, which has a capacity of 700 million barrels of oil, contained over 550 million barrels of oil as of 2002. In 2001, President Bush directed the Secretary of Energy to increase the SPR up to its maximum capacity.

Strip-and-Gore Doctrine.

Property law doctrine followed in many states which provides that when a person conveys a parcel of property, the person does not intend to reserve an interest in a narrow, adjoining strip of land when that strip is no longer of use because of the conveyance. The deed, however, may explicitly reserve an interest in this strip of land.

Stroke.

See Metabolic Syndrome.

Stun Belt.

Electronic device worn under clothing which provides a debilitating electric shock when activated by remote control. Controversy exists over the use of this device to restrain disruptive individuals in court. Proponents assert that the stun belt is less restrictive and less obvious than handcuffs or leg irons. Opponents claim that the device causes the restrained individual to constantly fear its accidental activation or activation by the person holding the remote control in response to innocent activity which appears to be threatening.

Sudden Infant Death Syndrome [update].

The efforts of the SIDS network has reduced the number of SIDS deaths by 52% from 1990 to 2000 down to approximately 2,500 per year.

Sudden-Wealth Syndrome.

Variety of problems which may accompany the rapid acquisition of unexpected wealth by means of inheritance, gambling, investments, or entertainment careers. Typical symptoms include social isolation, uncontrolled spending, and embarrassing conduct.

Superlative Consumer Price Index; *Chain Consumer Price Index.*

Index designed to be more representative of how consumers actually purchase items than the Consumer Price Index. This index reacts to how individuals purchase more of a lower-priced product if another product increases in price. For example, a consumer may purchase more cabbage if lettuce goes up in price.

See Consumer Price Index [main volume].

Syrup.

See Codeine Syrup.

Syrup Head.

Person who abuses nonprescription drugs containing dextromethorphan.

See Dextromethorphan; Robotard.

T

Tardive Dyskinesia [update].
Approximately 15-30% of all mentally ill patients suffer from this disorder.

Telecommuting [update].
Telecommuting has increased 17% since 2000, with approximately twenty-eight million Americans telecommuting at least once a week.

Temporary Worker Visa [update].
In 2003, the United States H-1B quota was 65,000.

Tendonitis [update].
See Thumb Tendonitis.

Teratogen [cited].
The definition in the second edition was quoted by Derek L. Mogck, *Are We There Yet?: Refining the Test for Expert Testimony Through Daubert, Kumho Tire and Proposed Federal Rule of Evidence 702*, 33 Conn. L. Rev. 303, 306 (2000).

Therapeutic Jurisprudence.
System of special dockets, often including drug and mental health courts, in which non-violent offenders who have committed minor crimes have the option of either treatment or prison time. Under judicial supervision, care providers work with law enforcement to make sure the offender gets treatment. After the offender completes treatment, the charges may be dropped. Therapeutic jurisprudence emphasizes rehabilitation rather than punishment.

Thermal Imager [update].
In the case of *Kyllo v. United States*, 533 U.S. 27 (2001), the United States Supreme Court held that the use of thermal imaging to measure heat emanating from the home constitutes a search under the Fifth Amendment.

Thimerosal.
Preservative used to prevent contamination of vaccines and other products. Use of thimerosal is controversial because its high mercury content has been implicated in a variety of ailments including autism.

Thumb Tendonitis.
Tendonitis of the thumb which may be caused by using the thumb to type on small electronic devices.

Three Strikes Sentencing [update].
The United States Supreme Court determined that California's three strikes law does not violate the Eighth Amendment's ban on cruel and unusual punishment even though it may trigger lengthy prison terms for relatively small crimes. See *Ewing v. California*, 538 U.S. 11 (2003) and *Lockyer v. Andrade*, 538 U.S. 63 (2003).

Tiny Brother.
Privately owned surveillance cameras, as contrasted to cameras monitored by governmental

monitor the conduct of individuals at locations such as stores, parking lots, the workplace, etc.

Torpedo Stock.
Stock in a stock portfolio which performs especially poorly and has a substantial negative impact on the portfolio's value.

Torpedo Tax.
Income tax imposed on Social Security benefits. If a person receiving Social Security benefits has additional income, that income may cause an additional portion of the person's Social Security benefits to be subject to tax. Consequently, the marginal rate of the income tax may be as high as 50% which is greater than the highest normal income tax rate.

Tort Tax.
Alleged increase in the cost of products and services due to excessive awards to plaintiffs in personal injury lawsuits.

Toxoplasmosis [update].
More than 60 million Americans are thought to carry the *Toxoplasma* parasite.

Trace-Detection Device.
Machine which detects small amounts of explosive materials. These devices are frequently used at airports to screen passengers and luggage.

Trustafarian.
Person who is able to live a bohemian lifestyle without working because the person is a beneficiary of a trust supplying ample funds for support.
See Trust Slug.

Trust Slug.
Person who is unmotivated and lazy because the person is a beneficiary of a trust supplying ample funds for support.
See Trustafarian.

Tuberculosis [update].
Cases of tuberculosis in the United States dropped 45% from 1992 to 2000. Despite the drop of cases in the United States, more than 22,000 cases of tuberculosis are reported each year and an estimated 10 to 15 million Americans are affected with the TB germ with the potential of developing TB later in life. In 1998, the FDA approved a new drug, ***rifapentine (Priftin)***, for use in fighting TB.

Turbulence.
See Clear Air Turbulence; Extreme Turbulence; Light Turbulence; Mechanical Turbulence; Moderate Turbulence, Severe Turbulence

Turing Test.
Experiment in which a human must determine if he or she is dealing with another human or a computer by exchanging information with the entity. The experiment is designed

to determine if a computer can display human-like intelligence by convincing a human that the computer is actually human. The test is named after Alan Turing, a British mathematician.

See Reverse Turing Test.

U

UAV.

See Unmanned Aerial Vehicle.

Ultra-Wideband Technology [update].

The Federal Communications Commission approved limited use of UWB technology in February 2002.

Undercover Marketing; *Roach Bait; Under-the-Radar Marketing.*

Marketing scheme in which persons in collusion with the seller of a product make favorable statements about the product to induce others to purchase. People exposed to these verbal or written statements may purchase the product based on this allegedly unbiased and unsolicited praise.

Underride Litigation.

Lawsuit resulting from injuries caused when a vehicle rear-ends a tractor trailer and the trailer bed breaks into the vehicle's passenger compartment because the vehicle's hood is lower than the trailer bed causing the front of the vehicle to slip under the trailer bed. Many underride injuries may be prevented if the tractor trailer has a proper rear-impact guard to keep the vehicle from going under the trailer bed. The United States Department of Transportation regulates the use of rear-impact guards.

Under-the-Radar Marketing.

See Undercover Marketing.

Uniform Electronic Transactions Act [update].

As of 2002, more than 40 states have enacted some version of the UETA.

Unmanned Aerial Vehicle; UAV.

Pilotless aircraft flown by remote control. UAVs are frequently used by the military as surveillance aircraft in areas where it is too dangerous to send personnel. Some UAVs are also equipped with rockets or missiles which may be remotely launched.

Urban Legend.

Enticing story passed on from person to person by conversation, letter, telephone, e-mail, etc. which may have been originally based on fact but which has developed into a story that cannot be substantiated but yet is related as truth.

V

Variant Creutzfeldt-Jakob Disease.

See Bovine Spongiform Encephalopathy [main volume].

Viatical Settlement.

See Life Settlement.

Vulture Trust; *Ghoul Trust.*

Abusive practice of using a young individual who is seriously ill and with a short life expectancy as the measuring life of a charitable lead trust. This technique causes the value of the charitable deduction to be artificially high because the amount of the deduction is based on the life expectancy of a person the same age as the beneficiary but in good health. The charity does not actually receive benefits for a long period of time because the measuring life ends within a relatively short period of time which terminates the charity's interest and causes the remaining trust property to pass to the designated non-charitable remainder beneficiary. The Internal Revenue Service has restricted this technique by requiring, in most instances, a close family relationship between the parties creating the trust and the measuring life.

See Charitable Lead Trust [main volume].

W

Wet; ***Fry; Illy.***
Marijuana or tobacco cigarette soaked in embalming fluid and then dried.

Wi-Fi.
See Wireless Fidelity.

Wiki.
Simple online database which allows users to freely create and edit the content of a page on the Internet using a web browser. Ward Cunningham is credited with developing the wiki concept in 1995. The term is derived from the Hawaiian word for quick.
See Internet [main volume].

Wireless Fidelity; ***Wi-Fi.***
Method of accessing the Internet without wires. An access point transmits the Internet data much like a cordless phone transmits telephone conversations. A properly equipped computer may then communicate with the access point. Concerns regarding the safety of confidential data transmitted in this manner may arise, especially in law office settings.
See Hot Spot.

World Trade Organization [update].
As of 2003, the WTO had 146 members.

World Wide Web [update].
There has been a steady increase in the use of the Web.